Margaret Cicley

Tapestries of Loves Charms.

A Hearts Petals.

Author: Margaret Cicely

Tapestries of Loves Charms

Margaret Cicley

Awaken The Goddess Within.

Open Your Heart to The Bouquets of Love.

Love all its Forms Your Petals Cups.

Love Indeed, Weaves Times Grace.

Such Beautiful Treasures Within a Hearts Space,

Claiming Big-Bites & Nibbles of Pure Delights

A Warm Fireplace, Fall in Love this Night.

Give Smiles & Joy Its Place.

A Place Upon the Mantel.

This Book Belongs

To

Signature:

A Gift Just for You.

Butterfly Kisses and A Hearts Rendavous.

Margaret Cicley

This Journal Takes You Down Trips of Memory Lane.

Your Journey, Your Love, Your Passions &Fames.

How Well Have You Loved?

How Do You Love?

What Do You Love?

Who Do You Love?

Why Do You Love?

One Can Love in Many Ways.

With Loves Heartaches, Ribbon's & Their Frays.

Fall In Love All Over Again Take a Walk Down Memory Lane and Dance Your Way Back to Love.

Tapestries of Loves Charms

Love Is a Grand Teacher.

You Hold the Key.

Margaret Cicley

Write about A Loves Spell.

Tapestries of Loves Charms

Margaret Cicley

Write about A Loves Regret.

.

Tapestries of Loves Charms

Margaret Cicley

Write about A Loves Gamble.

Tapestries of Loves Charms

Margaret Cicley

Write about A Love of a Lifetime.

Tapestries of Loves Charms

Margaret Cicley

Write about a Love at First Sight.

Tapestries of Loves Charms

Margaret Cicley

Write about a Love Time Never Minded.

Tapestries of Loves Charms

Margaret Cicley

Write about A Soul You Love Just Because.

Tapestries of Loves Charms

Margaret Cicley

Write about A Love Your Heart Belongs Too.

Tapestries of Loves Charms

Margaret Cicley

Write about The Very Last Time You Fell in Love.

Tapestries of Loves Charms

Margaret Cicley

Write about A Past life Love.

Tapestries of Loves Charms

Margaret Cicley

Write about A Love Your Heart Skipped a Beat.

Tapestries of Loves Charms

Margaret Cicley

Write about A Timeless Love.

Tapestries of Loves Charms

Margaret Cicley

Love Beats Everyone to The Punch.

Be Open to Love.

Love Changes Everything.

Write about A Love That Stopped Time.

Margaret Cicley

Write about A Loves Daydream.

Margaret Cicley

Write about A Loves Scars.

Margaret Cicley

Write about A Loves Whispers.

Margaret Cicley

Write about a Loves Compromise.

Margaret Cicley

Write about A Loves Promises.

Margaret Cicley

Write about A Loves Forgiveness.

Margaret Cicley

Write about A Loves Burdens.

Margaret Cicley

Tapestries of Loves Charms

Write about Loves Kisses.

Margaret Cicley

Write about A Savage Love.

Margaret Cicley

Tapestries of Loves Charms

Write about A Sultry Love.

Margaret Cicley

Write about An Envy's Love.

Margaret Cicley

Write about A Cruel Love.

Margaret Cicley

Write about A Bitter Love.

Margaret Cicley

Write about A Seasons Love.

Margaret Cicley

Write about A Conditional Love.

Margaret Cicley

Write about An Unconditional Love.

Margaret Cicley

Write about A Guilty Love.

Margaret Cicley

Write about A Resentful Love.

Margaret Cicley

Write about A Pure Love.

Margaret Cicley

Write about A Secret Love.

Margaret Cicley

Tapestries of Loves Charms

Write about A Dreams Love.

Margaret Cicley

Write about A Tainted Love.

Margaret Cicley

A Write about A Spicy Love.

Margaret Cicley

Write about A Betrayal's Love.

Margaret Cicley

Write about A Familiar Love.

Margaret Cicley

Write about A Complicated Love.

Margaret Cicley

Write about A Forbidden Love.

Margaret Cicley

Write about An Impossible Love.

Margaret Cicley

Write about A Cherished Love.

Margaret Cicley

Write about An Invitation for Love.

Margaret Cicley

"Sour Love & Boxing Gloves You Gotta Let It Go"

Margaret Cicley

Write about Making Love.

Tapestries of Loves Charms

Margaret Cicley

Write about The Sweetness of Love.

Tapestries of Loves Charms

Margaret Cicley

Write about A Seasons Love.

Tapestries of Loves Charms

Margaret Cicley

Write about A Springtime Love.

Tapestries of Loves Charms

Margaret Cicley

Write about An Autumns Chance Love.

Tapestries of Loves Charms

Margaret Cicley

Write about A Summers Love.

Tapestries of Loves Charms

Margaret Cicley

Write about A Loves Broken Engagement.

Tapestries of Loves Charms

Margaret Cicley

Write about A Lost Love.

Tapestries of Loves Charms

Margaret Cicley

Write about A Spiritual Love.

Tapestries of Loves Charms

Margaret Cicley

Write about A Sentimental Love.

Tapestries of Loves Charms

Margaret Cicley

Write about A Love That You Burn For.

Tapestries of Loves Charms

Margaret Cicley

Do You Remember These?

You Be the King & I Will Be the Queen.
We Will Live in A Castle Where Magic Is Seen.

You Can Fall from The Cliffs of Dover.
You Can Fall from The Heavens Above.
The Biggest Fall You Will Ever Make
Is
When You Fall in Love.

Rose Are Red Violets Are Blue
Sugar Is Sweet and So Are You.
Fall in Love with You.

Now Write One More Love Letter.
The Perfect Love Letter to Yourself.
One That You Would Expect to Receive.
The Finest Love Letter Ever.
And Don't Cheat Yourself.
Go for The Gusto.

You Are Loved Even If
You Don't Know It.

One Must Follow the Ease of Trust.
A Knowing's Whisper that Settles
The Dust.
Love Always Finds You.

Margaret Cicley

Your Love Letter.

Tapestries of Loves Charms

Margaret Cicley

Tapestries of Loves Charms

Margaret Cicley

Be Brave Be Bold

You Will Need Another Teacup.

Love Never Follows the Rules.
Love Takes on A Life of Its Own.

You've Gotta Give a Little Magic.

You've Gotta Take a Little Magic.

You've Gotta Be a Little Magic.

A Little Magic

Is

All You Need.

Margaret Cicley

More Books by Author: Margaret Cicley. © Copyright 2021 (Charmed Teapot Collection for Adults)

1. Charmed Mystics Muse "Dancing in Her Shoes"

2. Charmed Cottage Gold, "The Gift of Healing"

3. Charmed Cottage Teapot "Scrolls of Wisdom."

4. Charmed Cottage "A Rosey Heart"

5. Charmed Cottage "Pearls of Wisdom"

6. Charmed Cottage "A Diamonds Pearls"

7. Charmed Cottage "Aromas of The Heart"

8. Charmed Cottage "Airs and Graces"

9. Charmed Cottage "Whimsy" Footloose & Fancy-Free

10. Charmed Cottage "Romance with Panache"

11. Charmed Cottage Teapot. "Gifts of Practical Magic"

. 12. Charmed Teapot Mystic, & Her "Celestial Home".

13. Charmed Cottage Beautiful Moments & Cameo Moons"

. 14. Charmed Cottage "Artiste" Feast A Banquets Day.

15. Charmed Cottage Teapot, "The Alchemists Brew"

16. Tapestries of Loves Charm. "A Hearts Petals" (Journal)

17. A Mothers Wisdom and A Fathers Gold. (Journal)

18. The Soul of Home "A Hearts Fables & Songs"

19. The Lady of the Manor & Her Charmed Cottage Dream

.20. Find Someone or Something to Love.

21.Mother Nature's Recipes "The Bittersweet Teas Lavenders of Life"

22. Charmed Cottage Essence, "Awaken" Soul Stars

.

Our Charmed Teacup Collection for Children Coming Soon.

Margaret Cicley

ABOUT THE AUTHOR: MARGARET CICLEY

Charmed Mystic.

Margaret was born and raised in England, later emigrated to Canada. A Gifted Clairvoyant and Soul Whisperer Her gifts have inspired & guided her through life's measures.

Margaret connects to spirit effortlessly. Her Mediumship gifts have grown in leaps and bounds. She dances in and out of the spiritual and earthly domains often.

Margaret has written many spiritual books and hopes to open her healing centers. Having worked for over 3 centuries practicing knowledge acquired from her guides and their teachings, as well as her students. She Has Mastered her gifts splendidly, and her guides love her so. HA-HA. I Love Them Too.

Blessed Are We All.

Margaret Cicley

Charmed Cottage Corp

Website: www.charmedcottagecorp.com

Email: info@charmedcottagecorp.co

Made in the USA
Columbia, SC
08 November 2022